POETRY FOR KIDS

Robert Frost

~ POETRY FOR KIDS ~

Robert Frost

EDITED BY JAY PARINI
ILLUSTRATED BY
MICHAEL PARASKEVAS

MoonDance

Brimming with creative inspiration, how-to projects, and useful information to enrich your everyday life, Quarto Knows is a favorite destination for those pursuing their interests and passions. Visit our site and dig deeper with our books into your area of interest: Quarto Creates, Quarto Cooks, Quarto Homes, Quarto Lives, Quarto Drives, Quarto Explores, Quarto Gifts, or Quarto Kids.

First Published in 2017 by MoonDance Press, an imprint of The Quarto Group.
26391 Crown Valley Parkway, Suite 220, Mission Viejo, CA 92691, USA.
T (949) 380-7510 **F** (949) 380-7575 **www.QuartoKnows.com**

MoonDance Press titles are also available at discount for retail, wholesale, promotional, and bulk purchase. For details, contact the Special Sales Manager by email at specialsales@quarto.com or by mail at The Quarto Group, Attn: Special Sales Manager, 100 Cummings Center, Suite 265D, Beverly, MA 01915, USA.

ISBN: 978-1-63322-220-5

Library of Congress Cataloging-in-Publication Data

Names: Frost, Robert, 1874-1963, author. | Parini, Jay, editor. | Paraskevas, Michael, 1961- illustrator.
Title: Poetry for Kids : Robert Frost / edited by Jay Parini ; illustrated by Michael Paraskevas.
Description: Lake Forest, CA : MoonDance Press, [2017] | Series: Poetry for Kids
Identifiers: LCCN 2017010647 | ISBN 9781633222205 (hardback)
Subjects: | BISAC: JUVENILE NONFICTION / Poetry / General. | JUVENILE NONFICTION / Biography & Autobiography / Literary. | JUVENILE NONFICTION / People & Places / United States / General.
Classification: LCC PS3511.R94 A6 2017 | DDC 811/.52--dc23
LC record available at https://lccn.loc.gov/2017010647

Cover design and layout by Melissa Gerber

Printed in China
10 9 8

MIX
Paper from
responsible sources
FSC® C016973

Contents

Introduction

Robert Frost (1874–1963) once said that a poem should "begin in delight and end in wisdom." Frost's poems are both delightful—full of humor and high spirits—and wise. They often deliver a nugget of truth that stays with you long after you put the poem down.

Frost's poems are usually set in northern New England, especially in New Hampshire and Vermont, where he lived on farms throughout his long life. Unsurprisingly, his best poems deal with the everyday work of farm labor. They focus on such tasks as sowing seeds in the ground in springtime, mowing a hayfield at the end of summer, and picking apples in the fall.

Frost believed strongly in metaphor—that is, saying one thing in terms of another. For example, in the poem "Mowing," he uses the language of harvesting crops (describing mowing wheat and setting it in the sun to ripen) to talk about feelings and writing poetry. When the poet harvests the emotions of a time period, he cuts them down, bundles them into lines or stanzas, and allows the hay "to make." Almost any of the poems in this collection can be read as a metaphor. Frost writes simply about a task or a situation and invites you to think in wider terms about the image or idea that centers the poem.

Frost was born in San Francisco, California, and lived there with his parents and his sister until he was eleven years old, when his father died. He then moved with his family to Massachusetts, where he attended high school. After an early marriage and two attempts at college, he settled on a farm in Derry, New Hampshire. There he and his wife, Elinor, raised chickens and four young children.

Frost loved going to the general store in town, where he listened to farmers tell stories. He quickly saw that there was poetry in their lively way of talking. He learned to listen for the beauty in ordinary speech, what he called "the sound of sense," which is the music of language in conversation. Frost's poems became conversational, using simple words but combining them in ways that made them extremely memorable. For example, in "Stopping by Woods on a Snowy Evening," he writes about the wind blowing over the snow through the night woods: "The only other sound's the sweep / Of easy wind and downy flake."

Few other poets have captured the lives of ordinary people, their dreams and fears, their joy and grief, as succinctly as Robert Frost. His poetry remains a vivid testament to the wonders of nature, the pleasures and pains of farming, and the importance of poetic language as a way of framing experience and underscoring the work of thought and feeling in the creation of life itself.

The Pasture

I'm going out to clean the pasture spring;
I'll only stop to rake the leaves away
(And wait to watch the water clear, I may):
I sha'n't be gone long.—You come too.

I'm going out to fetch the little calf
That's standing by the mother. It's so young,
It totters when she licks it with her tongue.
I sha'n't be gone long.—You come too.

Totters — wobbles, wavers

A Late Walk

When I go up through the mowing field,
The headless aftermath,
Smooth-laid like thatch with the heavy dew,
Half closes the garden path.

And when I come to the garden ground,
The whir of sober birds
Up from the tangle of withered weeds
Is sadder than any words.

A tree beside the wall stands bare,
But a leaf that lingered brown,
Disturbed, I doubt not, by my thought,
Comes softly rattling down.

I end not far from my going forth
By picking the faded blue
Of the last remaining aster flower
To carry again to you.

Aftermath — what comes after

Into My Own

One of my wishes is that those dark trees,
So old and firm they scarcely show the breeze,
Were not, as 'twere, the merest mask of gloom,
But stretched away unto the edge of doom.

I should not be withheld but that some day
Into their vastness I should steal away,
Fearless of ever finding open land,
Or highway where the slow wheel pours the sand.

I do not see why I should e'er turn back,
Or those should not set forth upon my track
To overtake me, who should miss me here
And long to know if still I held them dear.

They would not find me changed from him they knew—
Only more sure of all I thought was true.

'Twere — as it were
Steal away — sneak away
E'er — ever

11

Ghost House

I dwell in a lonely house I know
That vanished many a summer ago,
And left no trace but the cellar walls,
And a cellar in which the daylight falls,
And the purple-stemmed wild raspberries grow.

O'er ruined fences the grape-vines shield
The woods come back to the mowing field;
The orchard tree has grown one copse
Of new wood and old where the woodpecker chops;
The footpath down to the well is healed.

I dwell with a strangely aching heart
In that vanished abode there far apart
On that disused and forgotten road
That has no dust-bath now for the toad.
Night comes; the black bats tumble and dart;

The whippoorwill is coming to shout
And hush and cluck and flutter about:
I hear him begin far enough away
Full many a time to say his say
Before he arrives to say it out.

It is under the small, dim, summer star.
I know not who these mute folk are
Who share the unlit place with me—
Those stones out under the low-limbed tree
Doubtless bear names that the mosses mar.

They are tireless folk, but slow and sad,
Though two, close-keeping, are lass and lad,—
With none among them that ever sings,
And yet, in view of how many things,
As sweet companions as might be had.

Copse — orchard or field
Dart — skip around
Whippoorwill — a small bird that sings at night
Mar — blemish

My November Guest

My Sorrow, when she's here with me,
Thinks these dark days of autumn rain
Are beautiful as days can be;
She loves the bare, the withered tree;
She walks the sodden pasture lane.

Her pleasure will not let me stay.
She talks and I am fain to list:
She's glad the birds are gone away,
She's glad her simple worsted gray
Is silver now with clinging mist.

The desolate, deserted trees,
The faded earth, the heavy sky,
The beauties she so truly sees,
She thinks I have no eye for these,
And vexes me for reason why.

Not yesterday I learned to know
The love of bare November days
Before the coming of the snow,
But it were vain to tell her so,
And they are better for her praise.

Sodden — wet
Fain — bound or determined to listen
Worsted — like a fabric
Vain — futile, hopeless

Stars

How countlessly they congregate
O'er our tumultuous snow,
Which flows in shapes as tall as trees
When wintry winds do blow!—

As if with keenness for our fate,
Our faltering few steps on
To white rest, and a place of rest
Invisible at dawn,—

And yet with neither love nor hate,
Those stars like some snow-white
Minerva's snow-white marble eyes
Without the gift of sight.

Congregate — gather
Tumultuous — bountiful or heavy
Keenness — interest, eagerness
Minerva —goddess of wisdom in ancient Rome

15

Storm Fear

When the wind works against us in the dark,
And pelts with snow
The lowest chamber window on the east,
And whispers with a sort of stifled bark,
The beast,
'Come out! Come out!'—
It costs no inward struggle not to go,
Ah, no!
I count our strength,

Two and a child,
Those of us not asleep subdued to mark
How the cold creeps as the fire dies at length,
How drifts are piled,
Dooryard and road ungraded,
Till even the comforting barn grows far away
And my heart owns a doubt
Whether 'tis in us to arise with day
And save ourselves unaided.

To the Thawing Wind

Come with rain, O loud Southwester!
Bring the singer, bring the nester;
Give the buried flower a dream;
Make the settled snow-bank steam;
Find the brown beneath the white;
But whate'er you do to-night,
Bathe my window, make it flow,
Melt it as the ices go;

Melt the glass and leave the sticks
Like a hermit's crucifix;
Burst into my narrow stall;
Swing the picture on the wall;
Run the rattling pages o'er;
Scatter poems on the floor;
Turn the poet out of door.

Hermit — a solitary man
Crucifix — a cross
Stall — room

A Prayer in Spring

Oh, give us pleasure in the flowers to-day;
And give us not to think so far away
As the uncertain harvest; keep us here
All simply in the springing of the year.

Oh, give us pleasure in the orchard white,
Like nothing else by day, like ghosts by night;
And make us happy in the happy bees,
The swarm dilating round the perfect trees.

And make us happy in the darting bird
That suddenly above the bees is heard,
The meteor that thrusts in with needle bill,
And off a blossom in mid air stands still.

For this is love and nothing else is love,
The which it is reserved for God above
To sanctify to what far ends He will,
But which it only needs that we fulfil.

Dilating — expanding, growing
Meteor — like a shooting star
Sanctify — make holy

Flower–Gathering

I left you in the morning,
And in the morning glow,
You walked a way beside me
To make me sad to go.
Do you know me in the gloaming,
Gaunt and dusty grey with roaming?
Are you dumb because you know me not,
Or dumb because you know?

All for me? And not a question
For the faded flowers gay
That could take me from beside you
For the ages of a day?
They are yours, and be the measure
Of their worth for you to treasure,
The measure of the little while
That I've been long away.

Gloaming — dusk
Gaunt — lean or haggard
Dumb — silent
Gay — brightly colored

Mowing

There was never a sound beside the wood but one,
And that was my long scythe whispering to the ground.
What was it it whispered? I knew not well myself;
Perhaps it was something about the heat of the sun,
Something, perhaps, about the lack of sound—
And that was why it whispered and did not speak.
It was no dream of the gift of idle hours,
Or easy gold at the hand of fay or elf:
Anything more than the truth would have seemed too weak
To the earnest love that laid the swale in rows,
Not without feeble-pointed spikes of flowers
(Pale orchises), and scared a bright green snake.
The fact is the sweetest dream that labor knows.
My long scythe whispered and left the hay to make.

Scythe — tool for cutting grass
Fay — imaginary fairy creature
Swale — low field on a farm

Going for Water

The well was dry beside the door,
And so we went with pail and can
Across the fields behind the house
To seek the brook if still it ran;

Not loth to have excuse to go,
Because the autumn eve was fair
(Though chill), because the fields were ours,
And by the brook our woods were there.

We ran as if to meet the moon
That slowly dawned behind the trees,
The barren boughs without the leaves,
Without the birds, without the breeze.

But once within the wood, we paused
Like gnomes that hid us from the moon,
Ready to run to hiding new
With laughter when she found us soon.

Each laid on other a staying hand
To listen ere we dared to look,
And in the hush we joined to make
We heard, we knew we heard the brook.

A note as from a single place,
A slender tinkling fall that made
Now drops that floated on the pool
Like pearls, and now a silver blade.

Ran — bubbled away
Loth — sorry
Barren — bare, empty
Staying — steadying
Ere — before

The Tuft of Flowers

I went to turn the grass once after one
Who mowed it in the dew before the sun.

The dew was gone that made his blade so keen
Before I came to view the leveled scene.

I looked for him behind an isle of trees;
I listened for his whetstone on the breeze.

But he had gone his way, the grass all mown,
And I must be, as he had been,—alone,

'As all must be,' I said within my heart,
'Whether they work together or apart.'

But as I said it, swift there passed me by
On noiseless wing a 'wildered butterfly,

Seeking with memories grown dim o'er night
Some resting flower of yesterday's delight.

And once I marked his flight go round and round,
As where some flower lay withering on the ground.

And then he flew as far as eye could see,
And then on tremulous wing came back to me.

I thought of questions that have no reply,
And would have turned to toss the grass to dry;

But he turned first, and led my eye to look
At a tall tuft of flowers beside a brook,

Turn — flip over
Keen — sharp
Whetstone — sharpening stone for blades
Tremulous — trembling
Tuft — bunch
Kindred — like a friend or relative
'wildered — bewildered

A leaping tongue of bloom the scythe had spared
Beside a reedy brook the scythe had bared.

I left my place to know them by their name,
Finding them butterfly weed when I came.

The mower in the dew had loved them thus,
By leaving them to flourish, not for us,

Nor yet to draw one thought of ours to him.
But from sheer morning gladness at the brim.

The butterfly and I had lit upon,
Nevertheless, a message from the dawn,

That made me hear the wakening birds around,
And hear his long scythe whispering to the ground,

And feel a spirit kindred to my own;
So that henceforth I worked no more alone;

But glad with him, I worked as with his aid,
And weary, sought at noon with him the shade;

And dreaming, as it were, held brotherly speech
With one whose thought I had not hoped to reach.

'Men work together,' I told him from the heart,
'Whether they work together or apart.'

October

O hushed October morning mild,
Thy leaves have ripened to the fall;
To-morrow's wind, if it be wild,
Should waste them all.
The crows above the forest call;
To-morrow they may form and go.
O hushed October morning mild,
Begin the hours of this day slow,
Make the day seem to us less brief.
Hearts not averse to being beguiled,
Beguile us in the way you know;
Release one leaf at break of day;
At noon release another leaf;
One from our trees, one far away;
Retard the sun with gentle mist;
Enchant the land with amethyst.
Slow, slow!
For the grapes' sake, if they were all,
Whose leaves already are burnt with frost,
Whose clustered fruit must else be lost—
For the grapes' sake along the wall.

Waste — blow away
Averse — against
Beguile — fascinate, draw toward
Retard — hold back

Reluctance

Out through the fields and the woods
And over the walls I have wended;
I have climbed the hills of view
And looked at the world, and descended;
I have come by the highway home,
And lo, it is ended.

The leaves are all dead on the ground,
Save those that the oak is keeping
To ravel them one by one
And let them go scraping and creeping
Out over the crusted snow,
When others are sleeping.

And the dead leaves lie huddled and still,
No longer blown hither and thither;
The last lone aster is gone;
The flowers of the witch-hazel wither;
The heart is still aching to seek,
But the feet question 'Whither?'

Ah, when to the heart of man
Was it ever less than a treason
To go with the drift of things,
To yield with a grace to reason,
And bow and accept the end
Of a love or a season?

Wended — weaved a way
Save — except
Ravel — bind together
Hither and thither — here and there

Mending Wall

Something there is that doesn't love a wall,
That sends the frozen-ground-swell under it,
And spills the upper boulders in the sun;
And makes gaps even two can pass abreast.
The work of hunters is another thing:
I have come after them and made repair
Where they have left not one stone on a stone,
But they would have the rabbit out of hiding,
To please the yelping dogs. The gaps I mean,
No one has seen them made or heard them made,
But at spring mending-time we find them there.
I let my neighbour know beyond the hill;
And on a day we meet to walk the line
And set the wall between us once again.
We keep the wall between us as we go.
To each the boulders that have fallen to each.
And some are loaves and some so nearly balls
We have to use a spell to make them balance:
"Stay where you are until our backs are turned!"
We wear our fingers rough with handling them.
Oh, just another kind of out-door game,
One on a side. It comes to little more:
There where it is we do not need the wall:

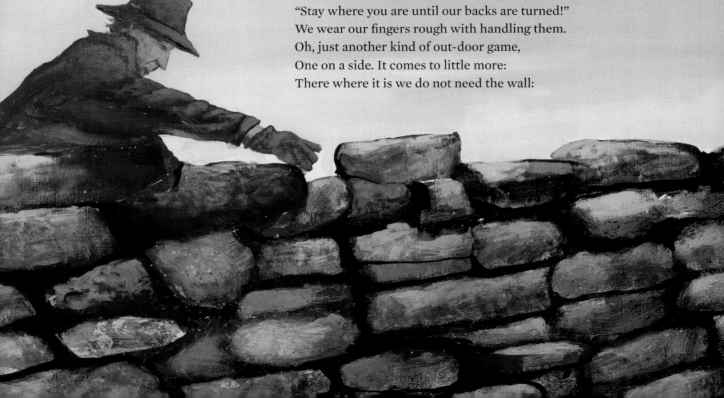

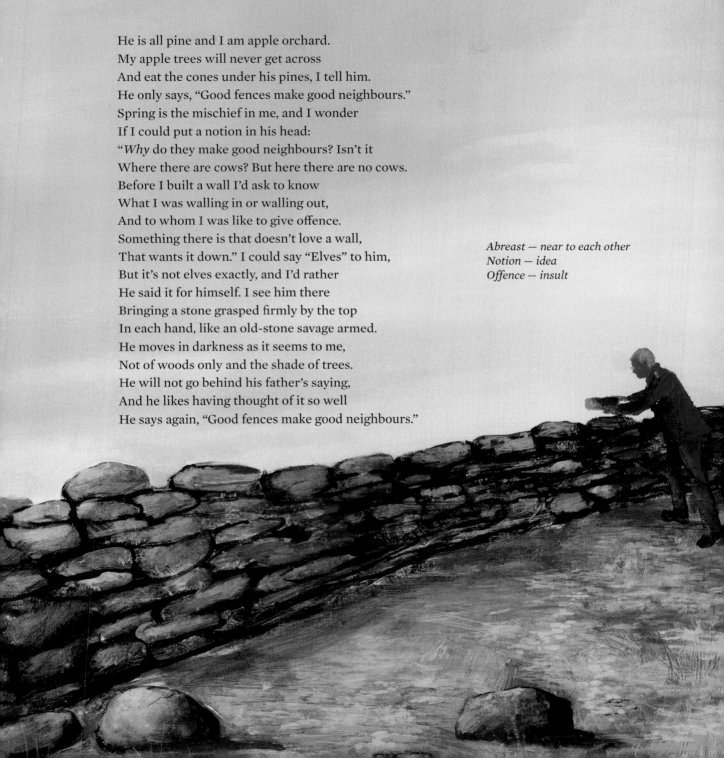

He is all pine and I am apple orchard.
My apple trees will never get across
And eat the cones under his pines, I tell him.
He only says, "Good fences make good neighbours."
Spring is the mischief in me, and I wonder
If I could put a notion in his head:
"*Why* do they make good neighbours? Isn't it
Where there are cows? But here there are no cows.
Before I built a wall I'd ask to know
What I was walling in or walling out,
And to whom I was like to give offence.
Something there is that doesn't love a wall,
That wants it down." I could say "Elves" to him,
But it's not elves exactly, and I'd rather
He said it for himself. I see him there
Bringing a stone grasped firmly by the top
In each hand, like an old-stone savage armed.
He moves in darkness as it seems to me,
Not of woods only and the shade of trees.
He will not go behind his father's saying,
And he likes having thought of it so well
He says again, "Good fences make good neighbours."

Abreast — near to each other
Notion — idea
Offence — insult

After Apple–Picking

My long two-pointed ladder's sticking through a tree
Toward heaven still,
And there's a barrel that I didn't fill
Beside it, and there may be two or three
Apples I didn't pick upon some bough.
But I am done with apple-picking now.
Essence of winter sleep is on the night,
The scent of apples: I am drowsing off.
I cannot rub the strangeness from my sight
I got from looking through a pane of glass
I skimmed this morning from the drinking trough
And held against the world of hoary grass.
It melted, and I let it fall and break.
But I was well
Upon my way to sleep before it fell,
And I could tell
What form my dreaming was about to take.
Magnified apples appear and disappear,
Stem end and blossom end,
And every fleck of russet showing clear.
My instep arch not only keeps the ache,
It keeps the pressure of a ladder-round.
I feel the ladder sway as the boughs bend.
And I keep hearing from the cellar bin
The rumbling sound
Of load on load of apples coming in.
For I have had too much
Of apple-picking: I am overtired
Of the great harvest I myself desired.

There were ten thousand thousand fruit to touch,
Cherish in hand, lift down, and not let fall.
For all
That struck the earth,
No matter if not bruised or spiked with stubble,
Went surely to the cider-apple heap
As of no worth.
One can see what will trouble
This sleep of mine, whatever sleep it is.
Were he not gone,
The woodchuck could say whether it's like his
Long sleep, as I describe its coming on,
Or just some human sleep.

Bough — branch
Trough — feed box for animals
Hoary — gray
Fleck of russet — speck of red
Stubble — bits of grass

The Wood-Pile

Out walking in the frozen swamp one grey day
I paused and said, "I will turn back from here.
No, I will go on farther—and we shall see."
The hard snow held me, save where now and then
One foot went down. The view was all in lines
Straight up and down of tall slim trees
Too much alike to mark or name a place by
So as to say for certain I was here
Or somewhere else: I was just far from home.
A small bird flew before me. He was careful
To put a tree between us when he lighted,
And say no word to tell me who he was
Who was so foolish as to think what *he* thought.
He thought that I was after him for a feather—
The white one in his tail; like one who takes
Everything said as personal to himself.
One flight out sideways would have undeceived him.
And then there was a pile of wood for which
I forgot him and let his little fear
Carry him off the way I might have gone,
Without so much as wishing him good-night.
He went behind it to make his last stand.
It was a cord of maple, cut and split
And piled—and measured, four by four by eight.
And not another like it could I see.
No runner tracks in this year's snow looped near it.
And it was older sure than this year's cutting,
Or even last year's or the year's before.
The wood was grey and the bark warping off it
And the pile somewhat sunken. Clematis
Had wound strings round and round it like a bundle.

What held it though on one side was a tree
Still growing, and on one a stake and prop,
These latter about to fall. I thought that only
Someone who lived in turning to fresh tasks
Could so forget his handiwork on which
He spent himself, the labour of his axe,
And leave it there far from a useful fireplace
To warm the frozen swamp as best it could
With the slow smokeless burning of decay.

Lighted — landed
Undeceived — made him aware
Cord — pile
Warping — peeling
Clematis — a plant

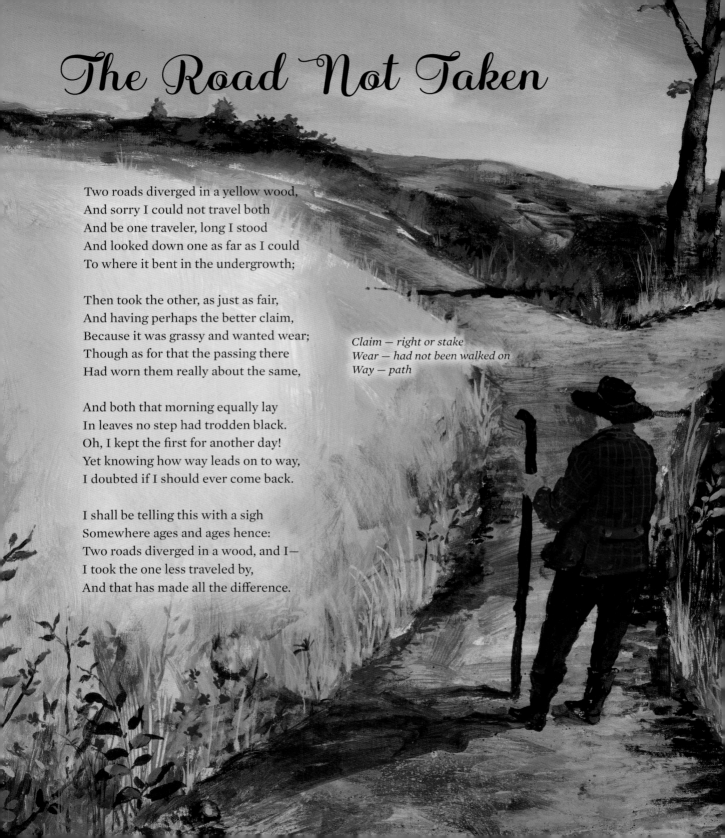

The Road Not Taken

Two roads diverged in a yellow wood,
And sorry I could not travel both
And be one traveler, long I stood
And looked down one as far as I could
To where it bent in the undergrowth;

Then took the other, as just as fair,
And having perhaps the better claim,
Because it was grassy and wanted wear;
Though as for that the passing there
Had worn them really about the same,

And both that morning equally lay
In leaves no step had trodden black.
Oh, I kept the first for another day!
Yet knowing how way leads on to way,
I doubted if I should ever come back.

I shall be telling this with a sigh
Somewhere ages and ages hence:
Two roads diverged in a wood, and I—
I took the one less traveled by,
And that has made all the difference.

Claim — right or stake
Wear — had not been walked on
Way — path

An Old Man's Winter Night

All out of doors looked darkly in at him
Through the thin frost, almost in separate stars,
That gathers on the pane in empty rooms.
What kept his eyes from giving back the gaze
Was the lamp tilted near them in his hand.
What kept him from remembering what it was
That brought him to that creaking room was age.
He stood with barrels round him—at a loss.
And having scared the cellar under him
In clomping there, he scared it once again
In clomping off;—and scared the outer night,
Which has its sounds, familiar, like the roar
Of trees and crack of branches, common things,
But nothing so like beating on a box.
A light he was to no one but himself
Where now he sat, concerned with he knew what,
A quiet light, and then not even that.
He consigned to the moon, such as she was,
So late-arising, to the broken moon
As better than the sun in any case
For such a charge, his snow upon the roof,
His icicles along the wall to keep;
And slept. The log that shifted with a jolt
Once in the stove, disturbed him and he shifted,
And eased his heavy breathing, but still slept.
One aged man—one man—can't fill a house,
A farm, a countryside, or if he can,
It's thus he does it of a winter night.

Clomping — stomping
Consigned — gave away rights
Charge — argument, claim

Hyla Brook

By June our brook's run out of song and speed.
Sought for much after that, it will be found
Either to have gone groping underground
(And taken with it all the Hyla breed
That shouted in the mist a month ago,
Like ghost of sleigh-bells in a ghost of snow)—
Or flourished and come up in jewel-weed,
Weak foliage that is blown upon and bent
Even against the way its waters went.
Its bed is left a faded paper sheet
Of dead leaves stuck together by the heat—
A brook to none but who remember long.
This as it will be seen is other far
Than with brooks taken otherwhere in song.
We love the things we love for what they are.

Groping — sneaking
Hyla breed — a kind of flower

The Oven Bird

There is a singer everyone has heard,
Loud, a mid-summer and a mid-wood bird,
Who makes the solid tree trunks sound again.
He says that leaves are old and that for flowers
Mid-summer is to spring as one to ten.
He says the early petal-fall is past
When pear and cherry bloom went down in showers
On sunny days a moment overcast;
And comes that other fall we name the fall.
He says the highway dust is over all.
The bird would cease and be as other birds
But that he knows in singing not to sing.
The question that he frames in all but words
Is what to make of a diminished thing.

Diminished — less than perfect

Birches

When I see birches bend to left and right
Across the lines of straighter darker trees,
I like to think some boy's been swinging them.
But swinging doesn't bend them down to stay.
Ice-storms do that. Often you must have seen them
Loaded with ice a sunny winter morning
After a rain. They click upon themselves
As the breeze rises, and turn many-colored
As the stir cracks and crazes their enamel.
Soon the sun's warmth makes them shed crystal shells
Shattering and avalanching on the snow-crust—
Such heaps of broken glass to sweep away
You'd think the inner dome of heaven had fallen.
They are dragged to the withered bracken by the load,
And they seem not to break; though once they are bowed
So low for long, they never right themselves:
You may see their trunks arching in the woods
Years afterwards, trailing their leaves on the ground
Like girls on hands and knees that throw their hair
Before them over their heads to dry in the sun.
But I was going to say when Truth broke in
With all her matter-of-fact about the ice-storm
(Now am I free to be poetical?)
I should prefer to have some boy bend them
As he went out and in to fetch the cows—
Some boy too far from town to learn baseball,
Whose only play was what he found himself,
Summer or winter, and could play alone.
One by one he subdued his father's trees
By riding them down over and over again
Until he took the stiffness out of them,
And not one but hung limp, not one was left
For him to conquer. He learned all there was
To learn about not launching out too soon

And so not carrying the tree away
Clear to the ground. He always kept his poise
To the top branches, climbing carefully
With the same pains you use to fill a cup
Up to the brim, and even above the brim.
Then he flung outward, feet first, with a swish,
Kicking his way down through the air to the ground.
So was I once myself a swinger of birches.
And so I dream of going back to be.
It's when I'm weary of considerations,
And life is too much like a pathless wood
Where your face burns and tickles with the cobwebs
Broken across it, and one eye is weeping
From a twig's having lashed across it open.
I'd like to get away from earth awhile
And then come back to it and begin over.
May no fate willfully misunderstand me
And half grant what I wish and snatch me away
Not to return. Earth's the right place for love:
I don't know where it's likely to go better.
I'd like to go by climbing a birch tree,
And climb black branches up a snow-white trunk
Toward heaven, till the tree could bear no more,
But dipped its top and set me down again.
That would be good both going and coming back.
One could do worse than be a swinger of birches.

Enamel — hard surface
Bracken by the load — ferns
Poise — balance
Considerations — worries

Putting in the Seed

You come to fetch me from my work to-night
When supper's on the table, and we'll see
If I can leave off burying the white
Soft petals fallen from the apple tree.

(Soft petals, yes, but not so barren quite,
Mingled with these, smooth bean and wrinkled pea;)
And go along with you ere you lose sight
Of what you came for and become like me,

Slave to a springtime passion for the earth.
How Love burns through the Putting in the Seed
On through the watching for that early birth
When, just as the soil tarnishes with weed,

The sturdy seedling with arched body comes
Shouldering its way and shedding the earth crumbs.

Barren — wasted
Tarnishes — rusts or is ruined by
crumbs [bits of soil]

The Cow in Apple Time

Something inspires the only cow of late
To make no more of a wall than an open gate,
And think no more of wall-builders than fools.
Her face is flecked with pomace and she drools
A cider syrup. Having tasted fruit,
She scorns a pasture withering to the root.
She runs from tree to tree where lie and sweeten
The windfalls spiked with stubble and worm-eaten.
She leaves them bitten when she has to fly.
She bellows on a knoll against the sky.
Her udder shrivels and the milk goes dry.

Pomace — pulpy substance
Bellows — shouts

"Out, Out—"

The buzz-saw snarled and rattled in the yard
And made dust and dropped stove-length sticks of wood,
Sweet-scented stuff when the breeze drew across it.
And from there those that lifted eyes could count
Five mountain ranges one behind the other
Under the sunset far into Vermont.
And the saw snarled and rattled, snarled and rattled,
As it ran light, or had to bear a load.
And nothing happened: day was all but done.
Call it a day, I wish they might have said
To please the boy by giving him the half hour
That a boy counts so much when saved from work.
His sister stood beside them in her apron
To tell them "Supper." At the word, the saw,
As if to prove saws knew what supper meant,
Leaped out at the boy's hand, or seemed to leap—
He must have given the hand. However it was,
Neither refused the meeting. But the hand!

The boy's first outcry was a rueful laugh,
As he swung toward them holding up the hand
Half in appeal, but half as if to keep
The life from spilling. Then the boy saw all—
Since he was old enough to know, big boy
Doing a man's work, though a child at heart—
He saw all spoiled. "Don't let him cut my hand off—
The doctor, when he comes. Don't let him, sister!"
So. But the hand was gone already.
The doctor put him in the dark of ether.
He lay and puffed his lips out with his breath.
And then—the watcher at his pulse took fright.
No one believed. They listened at his heart.
Little—less—nothing!—and that ended it.
No more to build on there. And they, since they
Were not the one dead, turned to their affairs.

Drew — moved
Counts — values
Rueful — sad
Appeal — hope
Ether — a gas that knocks you out
Affairs — business

Snow Dust

The way a crow
Shook down on me
The dust of snow
From a hemlock tree

Has given my heart
A change of mood
And saved some part
Of a day I had rued.

Rued — regretted

42

Stopping by Woods on a Snowy Evening

Whose woods these are I think I know.
His house is in the village though;
He will not see me stopping here
To watch his woods fill up with snow.

My little horse must think it queer
To stop without a farmhouse near
Between the woods and frozen lake
The darkest evening of the year.

He gives his harness bells a shake
To ask if there is some mistake.
The only other sound's the sweep
Of easy wind and downy flake.

The woods are lovely, dark and deep,
But I have promises to keep,
And miles to go before I sleep,
And miles to go before I sleep.

Queer — odd
Downy — fluffy and white

Tree at My Window

Tree at my window, window tree,
My sash is lowered when night comes on;
But let there never be curtain drawn
Between you and me.

Vague dream head lifted out of the ground,
And thing next most diffuse to cloud,
Not all your light tongues talking aloud
Could be profound.

But tree, I have seen you taken and tossed,
And if you have seen me when I slept,
You have seen me when I was taken and swept
And all but lost.

That day she put our heads together,
Fate had her imagination about her,
Your head so much concerned with outer,
Mine with inner, weather.

Diffuse — thinning out
Profound — important

Choose Something Like a Star

O Star (the fairest one in sight),
We grant your loftiness the right
To some obscurity of cloud—
It will not do to say of night,
Since dark is what brings out your light.
Some mystery becomes the proud.
But to be wholly taciturn
In your reserve is not allowed.
Say something to us we can learn
By heart and when alone repeat.
Say something! And it says, 'I burn.'
But say with what degree of heat.
Talk Fahrenheit, talk Centigrade.
Use language we can comprehend.
Tell us what elements you blend.
It gives us strangely little aid,
But does tell something in the end.
And steadfast as Keats' Eremite,
Not even stooping from its sphere,
It asks a little of us here.
It asks of us a certain height,
So when at times the mob is swayed
To carry praise or blame too far,
We may choose something like a star
To stay our minds on and be staid.

Loftiness — high position
Obscurity — hiding place
Taciturn — saying little
Reserve — holding back
Keats' Eremite — a star in a poem by John Keats
Stay — fix
Staid — made to feel solid

What Robert Was Thinking

The Pasture: This poem is an invitation to Frost's world of green fields, cows, and simple pleasure.

A Late Walk: After a day's work, with the fields mown, the speaker walks into the pasture and thinks of a loved one, for whom he picks a flower.

Into My Own: The poet asserts his own awareness of himself in the world, a place where he has a strong sense of his own values and disposition.

Ghost House: In this poem, a house becomes a representative of the poet's soul, a dwelling he recalls with nostalgia.

My November Guest: The poet thinks of his sorrow, which seems a constant visitor in November, as he looks forward to winter with some apprehension.

Stars: Stars have always fascinated poets, and Frost is no exception. This poem is a lovely meditation on the vivid lights that fill the sky on a winter's night.

Storm Fear: This haunting poem is about a small family that experiences the pounding wind of a storm outside their little house. They feel tremendously afraid. At the same time, there is strength in their family of three, and they can huddle together to overcome this fear.

To the Thawing Wind: The wind seems like a chaotic force in this poem, affecting the world, the house, the poet, and his poems. It scatters everything, and the poet celebrates this wild energy.

A Prayer in Spring: The poem is a beautiful prayer for a season that brings all sorts of bounty and promise, including white blossoms on fruit trees.

Flower-Gathering: This haunting poem is addressed to a loved one. It poses many questions, all of them concerning the bouquet of flowers that the speaker has picked.

Mowing: This remains one of Frost's best early poems. It's about mowing a field to make hay, but it's also about writing. The poet uses his pen to find things out about the world. It's how he pursued the difficult work of knowing.

Going for Water: As with many Frost poems, this is about a simple job. Going for water represents the human need for sustenance, for quenching our thirst. It is both a physical and emotional need.

The Tuft of Flowers: The speaker notices that a mower who has gone before him (and departed) has left a tuft of flowers out of sheer "morning gladness" at its beauty. The poet finds in this mysterious mower a kindred spirit and suggests that there is a common bond that unites people even when they work separately.

October: The seasons mean a great deal to this poet, who reads them closely, looking for signs that are emotional, spiritual, and physical.

Reluctance: Human beings are reluctant to let go of anything—love or a season that they love. This poem notices and celebrates that slight hesitation that everyone feels at times when the season has passed and one must let go of something very dear.

Mending Wall: The speaker summons a neighbor to walk along and repair a dry stone wall, putting back stones that have tumbled through winter. The dialogue takes place mainly in the speaker's head, and it brings out the idea of two worlds. Is the wall a good thing or a bad thing? The speaker is against walls. But he can't resist the old saying: "Good fences make good neighbors," which he puts in the mouth of the neighbor, who represents an "old-stone savage."

After Apple-Picking: Apple picking is an important part of the farming world; however, the speaker in this poem is talking about more than apples. The apples are poems to be picked and preserved, let to fall to the ground and rot, or to be taken away to be pressed into cider. This is a poem about the end of a day, weariness itself, and even the end of a life.

The Wood-Pile: In many poems by Frost, a solitary man goes into the woods and measures himself against the natural world. Here he goes into a swamp and discovers a mysterious cord of wood. Who would take such trouble, cutting and stacking so much wood in a place where it seems quite useless? Is this somewhat like writing poems, stacking the lines, which are measured out carefully and left, perhaps, for nobody to read?

The Road Not Taken: This is Frost's most famous poem, and it's about the classic "fork in the road." Notice that the two paths are "really about the same" in how worn they may be. The poem is a tricky one that needs to be read carefully. In the last two lines, the speaker declares that by taking one road and not another this made "all the difference." How can that be when "both that morning equally lay?"

An Old Man's Winter Night: This is an eerie poem about an old man who seems at the end of his life. He can't "keep" anything anymore. Not a house, not a countryside, not himself. It's a beautiful poem, too, with the stars looking in on the old man.

Hyla Brook: Many of Frost's poems are about inspiration, and the brook in this poem is about just that: inspiration that goes underground at times, hidden from view. Just as the brook will reemerge in flowers—jewelweeds—the poet's hidden inspiration will emerge as poetry.

The Oven Bird: An ovenbird is common in the woods of New England, but it has a rather flat chirping sound. It knows "in singing not to sing." The bird is like the poet who Frost imagines—who thinks about a world where nothing is quite like it used to be. Frost seems to identify with this bird and see his work as similar to that of the poet in the poem.

Birches: Boys in New England used to like to climb birch trees to find their tipping point, where they bend to the earth. The poet takes this a step further, building a whole story about the best place for love. Is it heaven or earth? The answer is clear: "Earth's the best place for love."

Putting in the Seed: In another of Frost's poems about work, the work of planting is important. The farmer puts the flower petals into the earth as fertilizer, but in this poem, the writer wonders about where the reward for this work lies. Is it in the act of putting the seed in the ground or watching the sprouts that will come later?

The Cow in Apple Time: This is a funny poem about a cow that breaks through a wall into an apple orchard and gorges on fruit that ferment in her stomach and upset her system so that she can't produce milk. The poem suggests that animals, including humans, never seem quite satisfied with what they have, and how yearning can produce ill effects.

"Out, Out —": This tragedy, which is about the accidental death of a boy on a farm at the turn of the twentieth century, actually happened in Frost's neighborhood. He was very moved by the story and recreates it with tremendous force. The poem is about—among many things—how poor farmers deal with the loss of a hand (which has multiple meanings). It's mainly a poem about death and how one deals with unexpected horrors like this.

Snow Dust: A little instance of movement in nature can shake a person into awareness. In this poem, snow is being shaken down to the ground and lands on the speaker.

Stopping by Woods on a Snowy Evening: This poem takes on the silence of the snowy woods, which are like eternity. It's a poem about not only death but also life and the need to press on even with miles to go before the speaker can lay down his head.

Tree at My Window: Here Frost contemplates "inside" and "outside." The speaker is inside the house, and the trees live outside the window. There is an urgent feeling in the poem that the speaker wants to join the tree, to blend his interior with his exterior.

Choose Something Like a Star: Poets often cast their eyes to the heavens, finding something in a star to fix on and help—a point of aspiration. This poem is a classic wish for something permanent, something that can lift us up in dark times.

index